Foreword

am very pleased that one of my first tasks as the new director of the Active Community Unit s to introduce this report.

This report provides a valuable addition to our knowledge of older volunteers, volunteering and government funded projects. I am sure it will be of great interest to older volunteers themselves, organisations that work with older volunteers and government. It will of course be of most interest to the actual projects that took part in the Initiative and the original members of the Older Volunteer Groups who met back in 1997.

Helen Edwards
Director: Active Community Unit

Acknowledgements

The study of a substantial and complex programme of work such as the Older Volunteers Initiative can only be accomplished with the help of a large number of people. As a result we have a number of debts of gratitude to acknowledge.

In the first place we would like to thank Duncan Prime, Louisa Carrad and Russell Todd of the Home Office. They shared our enthusiasm for the study, contributed a great deal to the development of our thinking and to the design of the project and provided practical help in accessing much of the information we needed.

Valuable contributions were made by the other members of the project team. Margaret Harris was a source of wise advice about data collection and analysis and helped us to present our findings with greater clarity, coherence and precision. Laura Keely not only assisted us with data collection but also made an important contribution to the analysis of a very substantial and varied body of material.

We had two opportunities to present work in progress and emerging findings to meetings of the Older Volunteers Liaison Group and we are grateful to the members of the Group for their encouragement and helpful comments.

Above all we need to thank the staff, volunteers and users of the 26 HOOVI projects for their willingness to spend time with us and share their experiences. Without their active co-operation we could not have written this report. We are particularly grateful for the trouble people took to ensure that we could meet them and the speed with which most of them responded to our initial contacts. The timetable for the fieldwork was extremely tight and its achievement only became possible because of this very active interest in what we are doing.

We were deeply impressed by the quality of the work that was being undertaken by many of the projects and by the imagination and dedication which volunteers and staff brought to the task. We hope we have communicated some of this enthusiasm and respect in the report.

Colin Rochester and Romayne Hutchison
Centre for Nonprofit and Voluntary Sector Management University of Surrey Roehampton

Colin Rochester is Director; Romayne Hutchison is Senior Associate Researcher; and Laura Keely was Research Assistant, Centre for Nonprofit and Voluntary Sector Management University of Surrey Roehampton.

Margaret Harris is Professor of Voluntary Sector Organisation at Aston University Business School.

Contents

Home Office Research Study 248

A Review of the Home Office Older Volunteers Initiative

Colin Rochester and Romayne Hutchison
with
Margaret Harris and Laura Keely

Home Office Research, Development and Statistics Directorate
June 2002

Home Office Research Studies

The Home Office Research Studies are reports on research undertaken by or on behalf of the Home Office. They cover the range of subjects for which the Home Secretary has responsibility. Other publications produced by the Research, Development and Statistics Directorate include Findings, Statistical Bulletins and Statistical Papers.

The Research, Development and Statistics Directorate

RDS is part of the Home Office. The Home Office's purpose is to build a safe, just and tolerant society in which the rights and responsibilities of individuals, families and communities are properly balanced and the protection and security of the public are maintained.

RDS is also part of National Statistics (NS). One of the aims of NS is to inform Parliament and the citizen about the state of the nation and provide a window on the work and performance of government, allowing the impact of government policies and actions to be assessed.

Therefore –

Research Development and Statistics Directorate exists to improve policy making, decision taking and practice in support of the Home Office purpose and aims, to provide the public and Parliament with information necessary for informed debate and to publish information for future use.

First published 2002
Application for reproduction should be made to the Communication Development Unit, Room 201, Home Office, 50 Queen Anne's Gate, London SW1H 9AT.
© Crown copyright 2002   ISBN 1 84082 850 1
                          ISSN 0072 6435

Summary

During the four years 1999–2003 the Home Office Older Volunteers Initiative (HOOVI) provided funding of £1.476 million to 26 projects aimed at improving the number and quality of the opportunities for people aged 50 or over to volunteer and involve themselves in the community.

Sixteen of the 26 projects were directly concerned with recruiting volunteers and involving them in many different roles and settings. Their experience demonstrated that older people from a variety of backgrounds could be attracted into volunteering if efforts were made to recruit them. It also showed that older volunteers could play their part in a wider range of activities than was expected of them.

The research also suggests that:

- organisations whose mission or purpose is to promote the well-being of older people have a considerable advantage in involving older people as volunteers

- the extent to which volunteering is a recognised and central feature of an organisation's work is an important factor in its ability to involve older volunteers quickly and effectively

- older people from black and minority ethnic communities with little or no tradition of formal volunteering are more likely to volunteer within their own communities than in "mainstream" organisations

- the contribution of older people is likely to be especially valuable in working with frail and isolated older people, intergenerational activities with school-age children and in helping other people with long-term health problems to manage their condition.

The Initiative also advanced the knowledge about older people as volunteers, identified and disseminated good practice and generally promoted the idea of volunteering by older people.

Guidance about good practice was developed in relation to:

- identifying and overcoming barriers to volunteering by older people

- support for volunteering by older and retired employees of local authorities

- encouraging volunteering by black and minority ethnic older people

- mentoring.

Vigorous attempts were made to disseminate good practice, and to promote the idea of volunteering by older people more generally, during the life of the programme. There was little evidence, however, that this work would be followed up in the longer term.

Learning the lessons

The Initiative provided important lessons about how to encourage and promote volunteering by older people. These included messages about:

- older volunteers – what they had to offer and what they wanted

- the obstacles to volunteering by older people – the policies and practices of volunteer-involving organisations; the attitudes of older people themselves; practical obstacles such as lack of mobility and money; and cultural barriers

- publicity and recruitment

- selection, induction, training and support of older volunteers

- organising the activities of older volunteers

- the wider organisational arrangements needed to support volunteering by older people.

Limitations of the Initiative

The HOOVI programme achieved a great deal not only in supporting projects that have promoted volunteering by older people and have addressed community needs but also in developing greater knowledge and understanding of how to involve older people as active members of the community. The design and implementation of the Initiative, however, had serious limitations which reduced its capacity to meet its aims. These were:

- it was essentially a reactive rather than a proactive approach. The programme was an aggregate of bids for funding from organisations with different interests and different agendas rather than being systematically developed to address a coherent set of aims and objectives

- much of the programme was made up of short term and small-scale projects with a limited capacity to lay strong foundations for continuing activity

- to a great extent the individual projects operated in isolation and had little opportunity to compare experiences.

Recommendations for volunteer-involving organisations

Vision and commitment
Organisations which aim to involve older people as volunteers need to:

- develop and articulate a clear and coherent vision of the rationale for involving older volunteers in the work of the organisation which identifies the expected benefits to the organisation and to the volunteers

- secure the commitment of the organisation as a whole including the governing body, the senior management team and those at operational level whose work will be affected

- consult the people outside the organisation whose co-operation and collaboration will be necessary if older people are to be involved in its work.

Planning

Organisations also need to develop concrete plans for a project or programme of activities. This involves:

- conducting an assessment of the needs which the proposed activities will address

- undertaking a feasibility study in order to be clear how the proposed programme or project can address the needs

- identifying the resources required to support the activities

- developing the structures and systems needed to support volunteering by older people

- setting out a realistic timescale for the establishment of the programme or project

- exploring the ways in which the work can be sustained in the long run.

Implementation

At the operational level organisations should be aware that:

- effective recruitment of older volunteers depends heavily on personal contact and the use of social networks

- successful contact with potential volunteers involves listening to what they are interested in doing and letting them know about the full range of possible volunteer roles open to them

- opportunities for volunteering by older people need to be flexible to take account of other commitments and open-ended to the extent that the volunteer can shape his or her role rather than simply slot into pre-conceived roles

- selection, induction and training should be appropriate to the role and context of the volunteering activity

- opportunities for volunteering should be as diverse as possible and not constrained by preconceptions of "appropriate" tasks for older volunteers

- attention should be given to identifying and overcoming barriers to volunteering by older people

- older volunteers are a valuable resource; the experience and skills they bring to the organisation should be recognised and valued.

Recommendations for government

There is a clear need for the promotion of volunteering by older people to be undertaken not as a "one-off" or on a project by project basis but as a continuing activity. This would involve:

- a cross-departmental strategy to promote the idea of older people as active members of the community

- active promotion at national and local level of volunteering by older people (this is the agenda of the Experience Corps)[1]

There is a case for strategic funding and support for two kinds of activity which projects funded under the Initiative undertook and which need to be built on over a longer period of time if they are to deliver substantial rewards. These are:

- volunteering by employees and former employees

- promoting good practice in volunteer-involving organisations.

The Home Office should identify ways in which they can work with other government departments and agencies to promote volunteering by older people in specific areas of policy and provision. These should include involving older people:

- as providers of services to other older people

- in intergenerational activities with schools

- as participants or leaders in developing active communities and neighbourhood renewal.

---

1. The Experience Corps is an independent non profit making company set up and funded by a grant from the Home Office. It started work in 2002 with the objective of encouraging people aged between 50 and 65 to offer their skills and experience to benefit others in their local communities.

Future funding programmes should involve:

- a more proactive approach by the Home Office

- greater realism about the resources and timescale needed to achieve major objectives

- building into the programme plan adequate and appropriate means of evaluating the work.

Recommendations for the private sector

Companies should be encouraged to seek the help of national and local intermediary bodies such as Business in the Community and local volunteer bureaux and councils for voluntary service to:

- develop an older volunteers strategy and code of practice

- make and sustain links with their local voluntary sector.

Origin and aims of the Initiative

The Home Office Older Volunteers Initiative (HOOVI) was launched by Mike O'Brien MP, the Parliamentary Under Secretary of State at the Home Office, in January 1999. Its aim was "to improve the number and quality of the opportunities available for older people to volunteer and get involved in their community" (O'Brien, 1999; 3). It was intended not only to make a significant contribution to the wider policy objective of encouraging "the giving of time and acts of community" (Home Office, 1999; 1) but also to play an important part in the celebration of the 1999 International Year of Older Persons (Home Office, 1999).

"For the purpose of this programme", said O'Brien, "older people' refers to those aged 50 years and over. So the programme will address a wide range of experience from those retiring early, or facing redundancy, to those who have been retired for many years; from those who are physically active to the frail and house-bound. Everyone has something to give if we can just make sure that they have the right opportunities and support" (O'Brien 1999; 3-4).

The ground for the Initiative and its launch had been prepared during the course of the previous year by a group of people drawn from the voluntary sector (organisations concerned with the well-being of older people and those which promoted volunteering), national and local government and business and the trades unions. Under the chairmanship of the Home Office Minister with responsibility for the voluntary and community sector (initially Alun Michael and, subsequently, Paul Boateng), the Older Volunteers Initiative Group had "come together to consider, develop and plan how best to promote and encourage volunteering by older people" (Home Office,1999; 1). In the process they had identified some specific aims for the Initiative. These were to:

- "instil the habit" (to increase the commitment of employee and retiree-supported volunteering)

- "bring down the barriers" (to remove the practical barriers to the recruitment of older volunteers)

- "catch the attention" (to ensure that volunteering opportunities were seen by older people and were attractive to them)

- "match the needs of the community" (to promote volunteering opportunities by focusing on specific community issues where there was a clear role for voluntary activity) (Home Office, 1999; 2-3).

In addressing its overall aim and these more specific objectives the Initiative had two aspects. In the first place it was intended to have a direct impact on the number, range and quality of opportunities for older people to volunteer and involve themselves in the community. In the second place but equally important, it was intended to provide the means of learning from the experience lessons which would inform future practice on a wider scale.

Implementation of the Initiative

This ambitious undertaking was delivered through a programme of grants to a variety of voluntary organisations. While the Home Office had developed the framework for the Initiative and set the terms for participation in it, its implementation was strongly influenced by the organisational goals and practices of the agencies which contributed to it.

There was, moreover, a significant degree of diversity among these organisations. In the first place they had different kinds of interests in the Initiative. These included a concern for the physical and mental well-being of older people, the promotion of volunteering per se, and the involvement of older people in a spectrum of activities which met the needs of people of different ages. In the second place they had different levels of resources and areas of operation. They included large national agencies and small community-based organisations.

The Initiative thus reflected the diversity of the participating organisations' interests and capacities. During the four years 1999–2003 it provided funding of £1.476 million to 26 projects. Because some projects involved a number of elements, it supported a total of 59 distinct activities. These included "one-off" publicity campaigns at one end of the spectrum and three-year programmes of work at the other. The average funding per project was £57,000 but the range was from £600 to £268,000.

An annotated list of the 26 projects funded through the Initiative is provided as Appendix 1.

The evaluation of the Initiative

In September 2000 the Research, Development and Statistics Directorate of the Home Office commissioned a team from the University of Surrey, Roehampton to undertake an evaluation of the Initiative. This study had two broad aims. These were to:

- assess the ways in which the Initiative had made an immediate or direct impact on promoting and encouraging volunteering by older people

- identify the lessons that could be learned from the experience and the ways in which they could be used to inform future practice and policy.

The task was to review the Initiative as a whole rather than individual projects. In any case many of the projects conducted or commissioned their own evaluations. The diversity of the activities involved, however, meant that the methods of data collection were tailored to the circumstances of each project.

Semi-structured personal interviews were conducted with the principal organiser or key informant in each project and a variety of methods were used to collect data from other informants. These included individual interviews face-to-face and by telephone (and, in one case, by e-mail), focus groups and observation. Information was supplemented and cross-checked from these sources with a variety of documentary sources made available by the participating organisations. Data were collected from staff involved in managing or running the activities; from the older volunteers involved in them; from the immediate users or direct beneficiaries of the provision; and from "secondary users" or "indirect beneficiaries" of the work (such as the organisers of day centres or residential homes in which older volunteers have worked).

In all 80 interviews (48 face-to-face, 29 by telephone and 3 by e-mail) and 13 focus groups were carried out during the period November 2000 to May 2001.

This report

In Chapter 2 the Initiative is reviewed and there is a discussion of the nature and extent of its achievements in:

- advancing knowledge about older volunteers and the opportunities for volunteering by older people

- identifying and disseminating good practice in offering opportunities for volunteering by older people and organising their voluntary activities

- generally promoting and publicising volunteering by older people

- developing new opportunities for volunteering by older people and involving older people in existing activities where they had previously been under-represented.

In Chapter 3 the lessons for good practice that have been learned from the Initiative as a whole are discussed. These lessons are about:

- what older volunteers have to offer

- what older volunteers want

- barriers to volunteering by older people and how to overcome them

- publicity and recruitment

- selection, induction, training and support

- organising the activities of older volunteers

- project development and organisational arrangements to support volunteering by older people.

In Chapter 4 conclusions are presented and implications spelt out regarding what has been learned for policy-makers and practitioners alike. The report ends by addressing recommendations for action by:

- organisations with an interest in encouraging and facilitating volunteering by older people

- the Home Office and other parts of the public sector

- the corporate sector.

2   A review of the Initiative and its achievements

Introduction

One of the initial aspirations was to measure the impact of the Initiative by collecting quantitative data about:

- the scale and scope of the activities created

- the numbers and demographic profile of the older volunteers recruited and the extent of their involvement

- the impact of these activities on the people who used or benefited from them and on the lives of the volunteers themselves

- the extent to which the older volunteers recruited under the Initiative continued volunteering after the Initiative had ended.

Shortly after the start of fieldwork it became clear that it would not be possible to collect adequate data of this kind. There were three reasons for this:

- Quantitative data were simply not available for collection and analysis. Some projects could not provide the necessary data: they had no baseline statistics and had not kept detailed records. Other projects which had kept records had used their own individual systems so that data could not be aggregated across projects. Projects ran to different timescales; at the time fieldwork was undertaken some projects had been completed or were close to completion, some were in mid-stream and others were in their early stages.

- In any case this kind of analysis could only be applied to those projects (16 out of the 26) designed to facilitate directly the recruitment and deployment of older volunteers and not to those which aimed to promote volunteering by older people in other ways.

- Quantitative techniques were not appropriate for assessing impacts which will be manifested in years to come but were unlikely to show themselves during the period of this fieldwork. Building a different atmosphere and changing people's perceptions of older people and the part they can play in voluntary action are very long-term projects.

It has not been possible to assess the impact of the Initiative in the quantitative terms originally intended. Even had this been feasible, it would have provided only part of the picture. This report is largely based on qualitative data and is structured to examine in turn the different ways in which the projects contributed to the Initiative's overall goal of promoting and encouraging volunteering by older people. The analysis of the fieldwork data has led to distinguishing four kinds of activity involved in the Initiative, each of these are examined in turn. They are:

- advancing knowledge about older volunteers and the opportunities for volunteering by older people

- identifying and disseminating good practice in offering opportunities for volunteering by older people and organising their voluntary activities

- generally promoting and publicising volunteering by older people

- developing new opportunities for volunteering by older people and involving older people in existing activities where they had previously been under-represented.

Advancing knowledge about older volunteers and opportunities for volunteering by older people

To an extent every one of the activities stimulated by the Initiative made a contribution to the advancement of knowledge about volunteering by older people; indeed, in Chapter 3 of the report there is an attempt to draw together a wider body of learning. The projects discussed below, however, made this a central objective for their work either as a foundation for the identification and dissemination of good practice or, more rarely, as an important activity in its own right.

While most of these activities focused on a specific area of volunteering, the study undertaken by the Institute for Volunteering Research (IVR) looked across a range of volunteer-involving organisations in order to identify the barriers that prevented older people from volunteering. IVR conducted a postal survey of 106 organisations, known from previous research to have operated upper age limits for volunteers, and followed these up with telephone interviews of 12 sample organisations. It published its findings (IVR, 1999) and distributed a summary to some 2,000 members of the National Centre for Volunteering (NCV), its parent organisation, and others. It also reported its main findings in Volunteering magazine and to the All Party Parliamentary hearings on volunteering and the Older Volunteers Liaison Network.[2]

As part of the National Association of Volunteer Bureaux (NAVB) *Increasing the Involvement of Black Elders* project, local volunteer bureaux carried out local mapping exercises of the ways in which black elders were involved in volunteering in their own communities and identified the barriers to their wider involvement in volunteering.

The NCV's *Mature Volunteers Enriching Resources in the Community (MAVERIC)* project focused on employer-supported volunteering (ESV) in local authorities. While the NCV staff had considerable knowledge of ESV in the private sector, they knew comparatively little about what was happening in local government where 30 per cent of its two million employees were over 50 and many were facing early retirement as a result of restructuring. The NCV's first task, therefore, was to conduct a survey of all local authorities. The findings have been made available through the NCV's website.[3]

The National Mentoring Network (NMN) conducted two projects concerned with the promotion of mentoring by government at the national level. The first of these was a mapping exercise involving interviews with 27 people from various sections of three government departments. It found that there was very little joint working between or even within departments (Drury, 1999). The second activity took the form of an "audit" of practice in 45 organisations which involved older volunteers as mentors (NMN, 1999). This used focus groups to explore quality issues in intergenerational mentoring: these highlighted some tensions between the older volunteers and the organisations with which they were involved.

Finally, Arthritis Care commissioned Coventry University to carry out an in-depth study of 22 older volunteers with arthritis who had undertaken training as lay leaders to deliver "Challenging Arthritis" courses. These were designed to encourage participants to become active agents in the management of their arthritis. By the time of the last interviews conducted

---

2. The Older Volunteers Liaison Network was a successor body to the Older Volunteers Initiative Group. Representatives of government departments, voluntary organisations, the corporate sector and trades unions have met on a regular basis during the course of the Initiative to exchange information and discuss related developments.

3. www.volunteering.org.uk

by the researchers, 14 of the participants in the study had led a course and had experienced significant improvements in health and self-esteem (Hainsworth and Barlow, 2000).

Identifying and disseminating good practice

In most instances the activities which advanced the knowledge about older people and volunteering paved the way for the identification of good practice.

The NCV's *MAVERIC* project developed a widely-disseminated good practice guide for local authorities. It "proposes the incorporation of volunteering in the structure of retirement preparation for local authority staff" and aims to demonstrate "how supporting volunteering is an essential part of any personnel officer's toolkit" (NCV, 2000). The guide was launched at four seminars for local authority personnel officers held in York, Exeter, London and Birmingham. Altogether 5,000 copies have been distributed to people working in local authorities and organisations which promote volunteering – including the members of NAVB, the regional organisations of the Retired and Senior Volunteers Programme (RSVP) and the Retired Executives Action Clearing House (REACH). The guide has also been publicised in the *Local Government Chronicle*, *Equalities Watch* (the organ of the employers' association for local government) and *Volunteering* magazine.

Similarly, IVR has published *Involving older volunteers – a good practice guide*. "The aim of this book" according to the introduction "is to look at why older people in the UK volunteer less than other people do, and what can be done about it" (Dingle, 2001; 1). Targeted at staff working with volunteers in the voluntary, statutory and private sectors, the guide reviews the contribution that older people are already making to the community and the obstacles to the greater involvement of older volunteers before suggesting how organisations could attract older volunteers, select and place them, and provide them with support and training.

NAVB's *Increasing the Involvement of Black Elders* project addressed the issues of good practice at two levels. Several of the local volunteer bureaux addressed local needs – by, for example, organising a co-ordinated recruitment campaign (Wigan and Leigh); the development of a black volunteering forum (Mersey); and a programme of positive action and outreach (Leicester). Nationally the experience of the project as a whole enabled NAVB to develop a set of guidelines and case studies (NAVB, 2000) which it disseminated to the 300 bureaux in its network.

The NMNs "audit" identified good practice in intergenerational mentoring which will inform the future work of the network and its members.

Similarly, Coventry University's researchers (for Arthritis Care) concluded that the "outcomes of the study can be of benefit to older volunteer trainers, to Arthritis Care in further developing their expertise with older volunteers and to other primary care groups involved in the management and care of people with arthritis" (Hainsworth and Barlow, 2000; 34).

In addition to these research-based projects, the Initiative also provided modest levels of support to two events convened by the RSVP which disseminated good practice. These were the *Leaders' Gathering*, a meeting for 150 volunteer leaders and staff, and a *Conference for the European Network of Older Volunteers*. The gathering provided an opportunity for volunteer leaders from different parts of the UK to exchange information and experiences and thus help to shape the future work of RSVP. The second event – attended by participants from 21 countries – disseminated research findings on ways in which isolated and lonely people could use information technology to improve the quality of their lives.

Promoting and publicising volunteering by older people

While it was suggested that, in general, all of the projects contributed to promoting and publicising volunteering by older people, in this section of the report, the focus is on the projects which had promotion and publicity as a key aim.

The UK Secretariat for the International Year of Older Persons Photographic Project had an ambitious remit which was broader than just the encouragement of volunteering by older people. This was "to help promote images of older people living active, independent lives and interacting with other generations", and it involved a travelling photographic exhibition; a photographic competition organised by Help the Aged (with winning entries on display in the exhibition); and a calendar for 2000 – "Towards a Society of All Ages" – which used some of the pictures from the exhibition.

The exhibition was launched in April 1999 and had been set up at 62 different venues by the end of March 2000 when the Secretariat was disbanded. The images were also made available to a much wider audience by means of a CD-Rom version. Ten thousand copies of the calendar were distributed to "key opinion formers" in every local authority and in business, central government and the media.

Assessing the impact of this kind of activity was practically impossible. As a proxy a telephone survey of a small sample of people known to have booked the exhibition was conducted and found that the exhibition had made an impression on the organisers and others taking part in these events. A typical response was "I remember it very well indeed – it was to show that older people can still lead active lives".

Northampton Volunteer Bureau received a small grant to meet the cost of printing 1,000 booklets and 250 posters which were widely distributed – in places such as libraries, churches and charity shops – around the town. This publicity was backed up by coverage in the local press at the time of UK Volunteers Week which included an "oldest volunteer" competition. There was no evidence that this modest "one-off" campaign had any effect on the number of older people taking up the opportunities for volunteering offered by the bureau, nor had this been the expectation. But it was found that there had been a very "positive response" to the promotional effort on the part of local voluntary organisations which involved volunteers in their work.

Some of the volunteer bureaux taking part in the NAVB's *Increasing the Involvement of Black Elders* project raised awareness about the under-representation of black elders in mainstream volunteering. They used a variety of methods including face-to-face contact with individual volunteer-involving organisations (both black-led and "mainstream" organisations) and convening meetings, forums and, in one case, a conference.

Business in the Community (BiTC)'s pilot *Time to Volunteer* project arranged meetings with representatives of 20 companies in two towns in the South East of England (Slough and Bracknell) to promote the idea of volunteering by retired employees and did follow-up work with five of them. This involved helping them form relationships with local voluntary organisations. While this low key Initiative did not produce dramatic results, it laid the foundations for a continuing relationship between some companies and local voluntary agencies.

The National Trust (NT)'s *Supporting and Developing Opportunities for Older Volunteers* project aimed to promote volunteering by older people by producing and disseminating an information pack aimed at employers and people who ran pre-retirement courses. While the pack publicises opportunities to volunteer with the NT – especially in conservation work, it also promotes the idea of volunteering more generally and includes details of other useful contacts. At the time of the fieldwork the pack had been completed but had not been printed or distributed. The plan was to produce 20,000 of the packs plus 150,000 leaflets and 2,000 posters for distribution through the NT's regional structures, initially in East Anglia and then across the rest of England, Wales and Northern Ireland.

Developing new opportunities

Sixteen of the 26 projects were directly concerned with recruiting and deploying older volunteers. In total they provided a rich diversity of experience in terms of the ways in which they sought to increase opportunities for volunteering by older people; the nature of the volunteering activities involved; the roles played by volunteers; the identity of the users of the service or the beneficiaries of their activities; and the characteristics of the volunteers recruited.

Approaches to increasing opportunities for volunteering by older people

Five projects addressed the Initiative's aim of "increasing the number and quality of opportunities available for older people to volunteer and get involved in their community" (O'Brien, 1999; 3) in one of three ways.

One – the Voluntary Service Overseas (VSO)'s *Tackling Global Disadvantage by Realising Older People's Potential* project – aimed to change the age profile of the volunteers involved in the organisation's existing activities.

Other projects – such as the Brighton Area of the Alzheimer's Disease Society's *Volunteer Befriending Scheme* or The Children's Society's Advocates for *Children and Young People* project – were designed to create new kinds of volunteer roles that could be played by older people and which would extend or enhance the work of the organisation.

Another set of projects – of which Pabulum's *Lifetimes* project and The Dark Horse Venture's Inside Out project were examples – developed new projects or activities in order to create opportunities for volunteering by older people.

Different models of volunteering

The 16 projects directly concerned with recruiting and involving volunteers promoted different types or models of volunteer activity:

- the first, adopted by more than half, followed the traditional philanthropic approach in which the role of the volunteer is to provide service to others

- the second of these overlaid elements of the service model with mutual aid or self-help approaches. Here the volunteers and the beneficiaries were drawn from the same communities or recruited through the same networks. Typically, users and volunteers were "learning together" and there was little distinction made between the roles of "user" and "volunteer"

- the third involved a community development approach where the objective was to empower users rather than provide them with services

- the fourth, adopted by two of the larger scale projects, was aimed specifically at facilitating the participation of older people in the political process

- the fifth, adopted by one of the two "political" projects, involved an overtly campaigning approach.

See Table 2.1

Activities undertaken by volunteers

The 16 projects promoted a number of different roles for older people. These included:

- direct work with users or beneficiaries such as befriending, advocacy, providing advice and information, providing care, teaching and youth work

- support roles including the provision of administrative and secretarial support

- practical tasks such as cooking and gardening

- leadership and managerial activities such as co-ordinating the activities of other volunteers, serving as committee members, assessing needs and developing new activities, public relations work and campaigning.

The projects offered activity in different fields as shown in Table 2.2.

Table 2.1:   Models of volunteering

Organisation	Project	Approach(es) to volunteering
Age Concern England	Activage	Service Mutual aid
Age Concern England	Age Resource	Service
Alzheimers Disease Society (Brighton Area Branch)	Volunteer Befriending Scheme	Service
The Children's Society	Advocates for Children and Young People	Service
Dark Horse Venture	Inside Out Project	Service
Help the Aged	Rural Initiative	Community development Mutual aid
Help the Aged	Speaking Up for Our Age	Campaigning Participation
MSF Union	Trades Unions in the Community	Service mutual aid
NACRO	Golden Years Activities Unit	Service
National Trust	Supporting and Developing Opportunities for Older Volunteers	Service
NAVB	Increasing the Involvement of Black Elders	Service mutual aid community development
Pabulum	Lifetimes	Service
Ravidassia Community Centre	Izzat and Seva ("respect and volunteering")	community development service
RSVP	Better Government for Older People	participation community development
Somali Women's Association and Welfare Group	Somali Women's Education and Training Project	service mutual aid
Voluntary Service Overseas	Tackling Global Disadvantage by Realising Older People's Potential	service community development

Table 2.2: Fields of activity in which older volunteers were involved

Organisation	Project	Field of Activity
Age Concern England	Activage	health promotion
Age Concern England	Age Resource	community education
Alzheimers Disease Society (Brighton Area Branch)	Volunteer Befriending Scheme	social welfare
The Children's Society	Advocates for Children and Young People	child protection
Dark Horse Venture	Inside Out Project	education
Help the Aged	Rural Initiative	social welfare health
Help the Aged	Speaking Up for Our Age	transport health social welfare environment
MSF Union	Trades Unions in the Community	Various
NACRO	Golden Years Activities Unit	crime prevention
National Trust	Supporting and Developing Opportunities for Older Volunteers	Heritage Environment
NAVB	Increasing the Involvement of Black Elders	Various
Pabulum	Lifetimes	community education social welfare
Ravidassia Community Centre	Izzat and Seva ("respect and volunteering")	community education social welfare
RSVP	Better Government for Older People	health social welfare education cultural activities recreation environment
Somali Women's Association and Welfare Group	Somali Women's Education and Training Project	community education social welfare
Voluntary Service Overseas	Tackling Global Disadvantage by Realising Older People's Potential	overseas development

The projects directed their efforts towards different users or beneficiaries. Six projects were concerned with older people as beneficiaries; two focused on the needs of children and young people and eight were not age-specific.

Table 2.3:   Users or beneficiaries of HOOVI projects

Organisation	Project	Users/Beneficiaries
Age Concern England	Activage	Asian elders
Age Concern England	Age Resource	isolated older people
Alzheimers Disease Society (Brighton Area Branch)	Volunteer Befriending Scheme	older people with dementia in residential care
The Children's Society	Advocates for Children and Young People	children and young people
Dark Horse Venture	Inside Out Project	various
Help the Aged	Rural Initiative	older people in rural areas
Help the Aged	Speaking Up for Our Age	older people
MSF Union	Trades Unions in the Community	various
NACRO	Golden Years Activities Unit	children and young people
National Trust	Supporting and Developing Opportunities for Older Volunteers	visitors to National Trust properties
NAVB	Increasing the Involvement of Black Elders	various
Pabulum	Lifetimes	frail and isolated older people
Ravidassia Community Centre	Izzat and Seva ("respect and volunteering")	Asian communities
RSVP	Better Government for Older People	older people
Somali Women's Association and Welfare Group	Somali Women's Education and Training Project	Somali women
Voluntary Service Overseas	Tackling Global Disadvantage by Realising Older People's Potential	people and communities in developing countries

Characteristics of the volunteers

The amount of information about the characteristics of the volunteers who were directly recruited by the 16 projects for this range of activities varied from project to project. While it was not possible to provide a full demographic profile some information could be presented about the volunteer population.

Age

Projects were able to provide very few statistics on the age of their volunteers. There were a number of reasons for this. In some cases the volunteers did not want to provide this information and, in others, information of this kind, if it existed, would be in the hands of a local group rather than the project organisers. Some organisations simply did not feel the need to ask.

The Initiative's definition of older volunteers as anyone over the age of 50 ensured that the age range of active participants was potentially very wide indeed. It included people in their 50s, who might still be in work; people in their 60s, who might have recently retired from full-time employment, and those in their 70s and older.

In nine of the 16 projects staff provided impressionistic and "broad brush" accounts of the age profile. The results are summarised in Table 2.4.

Table 2.4: Age range of volunteers

Age Range of Volunteers	Number of Projects
Only or mainly 50–59	3
Only or mainly 60–69	2
50–59 and 60–69	1
60–69 and 70+	2
Full age range	1
Total	9

Gender

There is a similar lack of data on the gender make-up of the volunteers recruited. According to information provided by staff in 14 of the 16 projects which were directly involved in the recruitment and deployment of volunteers:

- five of the projects had a majority of women volunteers (in one case 90%)
- two had a majority of male volunteers
- three had a reasonable balance of genders

- three reported that the gender balance varied from local group to group
- one was directed at women only.

Other characteristics
- Apart from the four projects which focused specifically on the black and minority ethnic community, the volunteers recruited by these projects were mainly white.

- Many of those recruited came from a professional or middle-class background but other recruits could be described as working class.

- What little evidence was discovered about recruits' previous experience of volunteering provides a mixed picture; many of the older volunteers recruited had been active in other voluntary roles in the past although there were several cases of groups who were new to formal volunteering.

The long term impact of the Initiative
The Initiative has thus stimulated a wide variety of activities. But to what extent will these continue to have an impact beyond the end of the funding programme? In some cases it was premature to attempt to make a judgement but, for most of the projects, one of three possible futures could be identified:

- activities involving older volunteers which have been established (or extended) as a result of agencies receiving funding under the Initiative will become an integral part of those agencies' activities

- work which was aimed at advancing knowledge, identifying good practice or promoting and publicising volunteering by older people has had an impact and much of it will continue to be developed, both by the agencies funded under the Initiative and others who benefited from the work

- continuation of some activities involving older volunteers and the opportunity to develop further or follow up some of the promotional work is uncertain and will depend largely on the availability of suitable funding.

There was very limited information about the extent to which individual volunteers were planning to continue their involvement. Given the high degree of commitment to their activities expressed by many, it was likely that most would remain involved beyond the end of the Initiative, provided that structures were in place to sustain and support their involvement.

Direct legacies

A number of organisations had continued to use the approaches developed during the Initiative to recruit and involve older volunteers. In some cases this involved an expansion of the activity. The extent to which they were able to maintain and expand these activities depended on their ability to identify and access alternative funding sources. The number of local Age Concerns involved in the work of Activage had been greatly increased with the help of funding from Microsoft, while the Dark Horse Venture was planning to extend the Inside Out project to other locations. Help the Aged had secured funding to continue to support the Speaking Up For Our Age programme, and the Somali Women's Association and the Alzheimer's Disease Society had identified ways of maintaining their work with older volunteers.

The wider impact of promotional work

There was evidence that many of the projects which aimed at promoting volunteering by older people by means other than direct recruitment and involvement had been built on and further developed both during and after the funding period. In some cases this had involved a wider impact on the work of the agency itself. The National Association for the Care and Resettlement of Offenders (NACRO), BiTC and the NT disseminated the lessons learned from their projects throughout their organisations so that these could inform other areas of work. The RSVP experience used the Better Government for Older People project to bring about changes to the ways in which it operated, such as undertaking more work with "non traditional" volunteers like those participating in the activities on Action Estates.

Other projects influenced the policies and practices of organisations other than those directly funded by the Initiative. The IVR continued to disseminate the findings from its research on age discrimination and plans to undertake further work on the issue. The NMN's work flagged up issues of intergenerational practice, influenced the development of mentoring in the probation service and raised awareness of the potential of mentoring projects. Arthritis Care planned to make available experience from its project to various national networks for the benefit of people with other long-term medical conditions.

An uncertain future

In the case of other projects which worked directly with older volunteers the future was less certain. Some had secured funding to enable them to continue some but not all of the activities supported by the Initiative. Others were looking for other sources of support with varying degrees of optimism.

As reported above, many of the Initiative-funded activities aimed at promoting volunteering by older people had left a legacy of continuing influence. For some of them, however, the evidence is harder to find. The UK Secretariat was wound up in March 2000 – three months after the end of the International Year of Older Persons. Without further funding, the host organisation, Age Concern England, was unable to continue to make available the photographic exhibition despite the fact that there was still a keen interest in booking it.

The NCV's MAVERIC project has made an impact; it disseminated information about employer supported volunteering widely among local authorities, and some of them were developing programmes and policies as a result. But the impetus gained by the project will be difficult to sustain in the absence of a dedicated member of staff at the NCV to take the work forward once funding under the Initiative has come to an end.

Following the review of the Initiative and its achievements, this chapter of the report will attempt to set out what the organisers of the projects have learned from the experience and what has been learned from them about good practice in promoting and encouraging volunteering by older people. Overall, this will involve an examination of:

- what older volunteers have to offer

- what older volunteers want – motivation and rewards

- barriers to volunteering by older people and how to overcome them

- recruiting older volunteers

- selection, induction, training and support of older volunteers

- organising the activities of older volunteers

- project development and organisational arrangements to support volunteering by older people.

What older volunteers have to offer

The IVR's good practice guide to involving older volunteers (Dingle, 2001) identified five features that make older people valuable volunteers. These are:

- *maturity* – older people have "lived through enough experiences" to enable them to understand the problems of others

- *skills* – they have also "spent decades perfecting all kinds of skills"

- *availability* – people who have retired from paid work or have finished child rearing tend to have more spare time and can be flexible about when they participate

- *loyalty* – older people spend more time on their volunteering and remain longer with their organisations than younger people

- *numbers* – older people make up an ever increasing proportion of the population and organisations cannot afford to ignore this important resource.

Ideas of this kind about the value of volunteering by older people were echoed by many of the staff, volunteers and users that were met during the fieldwork. As a project manager summed it up, "Young people are an asset but older people are a richer asset". Participants in the study supported the views set out by IVR in its good practice guide on skills – many older people were "educated and talented" and they had developed "life skills" and "people skills" as well as "professional skills" – and availability – older people had more time and could be more flexible. They agreed that maturity was an important asset and spelled out a range of qualities they associated with age and experience.

In their view the key qualities were:

- *Confidence and authority:* most informants felt that older people had greater confidence and more authority than younger volunteers. They had the confidence to "say if something was too much for them". They were "a force to be reckoned with; they're not slow to ask 'why is this happening?' They were ready to speak their mind and put forward their ideas about what should be happening because "they know these ideas will be taken seriously". They were able to manage their own activities. In one project, they were being groomed to co-ordinate the activities of other volunteers and nurture the younger ones.

- *Patience and tolerance:* a number of informants associated maturity with greater patience and tolerance. This was because older people were "older and wiser and more stable". They took "life at a steadier pace, they have time and patience and look at life more reflectively ... you're not throwing so many balls in the air; you're more relaxed". Their experience had also given them a calmer head and the ability to see more than one side of an issue. They were "less pushy" and they "knew how the system worked".

- *Commitment and continuity:* informants also associated maturity with commitment, continuity and reliability. Older volunteers were more tenacious; they showed greater willingness to see the job through to the end. Unlike younger people who might be looking to improve their CVs and career opportunities through volunteering, older people were more likely to be deeply interested in the activity itself; they were less selfish or more altruistic than their younger counterparts.

- *Membership of developed social networks:* informants suggested that older people were able to act as "ambassadors" for an organisation by using their extensive social networks and their membership of other organisations to promote its work and reputation.

- *Ability to engage with other older people:* informants involved in providing services to older people felt that there were significant advantages in involving older volunteers in their work. Older people found volunteers of their own age group "less intimidating" while the similarity of their experience meant that older volunteers were "on the same wavelength" as the users and understood them better. Older volunteers involved in educational projects were less likely to use jargon and had a better understanding of when to listen and when they needed to slow down, "As we get older we get mellow … you understand when the brain is slower". Older volunteers involved as befrienders of people with dementia, who were of their parents' generation, felt that they understood their needs better than younger volunteers.

- *Ability to engage with children and young people:* informants involved in mentoring projects and other intergenerational activities with schools and school-age children felt that older volunteers had qualities that equipped them for this kind of role. Older people brought a wealth of experiences of work and life which could offer young people a very different perspective. As grandparent figures they would provide a different kind of relationship. They could also exercise a "calming influence" on the children as well as providing the school with a new set of links with the local community.

Age Concern England: *Age Resource* Project
There were two advantages of involving older volunteers in helping older people get to grips with computers. Firstly they had more patience and were happy to spend time showing older people how to use the computer – unlike younger people who "just whiz and do it and don't really show how to do it". Secondly they were less self-centred: younger people may want to practise their skills whereas older people want to share skills.

What older volunteers want – motivation and rewards

Motivation – why did they come?

The volunteers that were met and the people who worked with them identified a variety of reasons why older people became involved as volunteers.

One group of reasons was to do with meeting the personal needs of the volunteers themselves. The most frequently mentioned and most compelling personal reason given for involvement was to fill a gap or a void in people's lives. Volunteering was for many a means of managing the transition from paid employment to retirement (and early retirement in particular); coping with a bereavement; or adjusting to the change brought about by older children leaving home and establishing independent lives. Volunteering kept people active and involved after retirement. One older volunteer described it as "a nice winding down way of doing things" until she realised that she had become so busy that she was "winding up".

Volunteering enabled older people to feel useful, valuable and "wanted". One volunteer underlined the importance of the activity to her sense of worth and well-being: "If it hadn't been for [the project] I would have shot myself."

Volunteering offered older people opportunities to meet new people and make new friends. Volunteering offered older people, such as the volunteers who shared their computer skills with other older people in the Age Resource project, a chance to "do something enjoyable" and interesting.

Finally volunteering provided older people with opportunities for personal development, including training. As one of the Somali Women's Association's volunteers summed up, "Everything is about learning" (although there was a difference of opinion about whether this should be accredited).

A rather different group of reasons for volunteering was to do with altruism. Indeed, one of the project managers suggested that older volunteers were "more philanthropic" than their younger counterparts who were often motivated by the desire to improve their CVs and their employability. Many volunteers felt that they had been fortunate and wanted to help others who were not so fortunate and to "put something back into the community". More specifically, some identified with older people and wanted to address their needs. Volunteers involved with the Alzheimer's Disease Society Befriending Scheme, for example, reported that they had been able to help people with dementia "feel wanted" and made them "feel a real person again". This identification with the needs of older people, moreover, was a key motivation for those involved in campaigning activities. Those who were active in the forums promoted by Help the Aged's Speaking Up For Our Age project felt quite strongly that issues affecting older people were not being addressed, and they had volunteered because they saw a "need for change" and they wanted to "make a difference". As some of them explained: "I felt pensioners were being let down" and "I wanted to fight for all the old people I drive".

Whatever the disposition to volunteer, however, people participated because they had been asked to do so. In many cases, the request or invitation had come from someone connected with the project – either someone already known to the new volunteer or someone they had met.

Rewards – why did they stay?

Informants identified a number of factors which determined whether older people, once recruited, would remain as volunteers. These were:

- *"keeping busy"*: older volunteers wanted to be active

- *the intrinsic worth of the activity:* older volunteers wanted to do something that they felt was useful and valuable. This was not only a question of the value of the contribution of the individual volunteer but also the quality of the achievements of the project as a whole

- *flexibility in the demands made on older people's time:* older volunteers wanted organisations to be flexible in involving them. Holidays and family commitments were important to older people and they needed to be able to fit their volunteering commitments around them. They also felt that their contribution to the organisation might need to change over time in line with changes in their interests, commitment and capacity

---

RSVP / Better Government for Older People Project: **Warwick Senior People's Forum**
Members said that they had gained "a lot of excitement and impetus", "a new outlet for skills", and renewed confidence after having retired and lost the status attached to employment. They valued the chance to network and gain contacts. They also enjoyed the opportunity to shape the organisation and develop their own interests through the forum.

- *willingness to give older people "real responsibility":* many older volunteers thrived on autonomy which allowed them to create and develop their contribution to the organisation rather than merely slotting into a preconceived role

> **Pabulum: *Lifetimes* Project**
> Members of the group said that they gained a great deal from their involvement with groups of older people and seeing their pleasure at trying a new activity or reviving a former interest: "You know you've done somebody some good and you feel good about life". They also referred to having regained confidence after taking early retirement and learned new skills that they were then able to pass on. Some wanted an opportunity to continue mixing with groups of people after retirement and to have interests outside the family, and felt they had achieved this.

- *opportunities to become involved in the policy-making of the organisation:* older volunteers wanted to be consulted and to feel that their contributions to decision-making were valued

- *opportunities for learning and personal growth;* older volunteers wanted to develop existing interests, engage with new ones and learn new skills

- *opportunities for social interaction;* older volunteers, often isolated at home, valued the opportunity to meet and socialise with other people

- *valuing the contribution of older volunteers:* older volunteers wanted respect, and the way they were treated had a major bearing on their commitment, how long they stayed and how much they contributed. Most appreciated being thanked and welcomed public acknowledgement of their contribution. However many older volunteers were not used to being valued and some gained confidence in their experience and skills which enabled them to make major contributions to the activities with which they were involved.

> **Age Concern Gateshead: Age resource**
> Volunteers felt that their efforts were appreciated and that they were never pressurised to do more than they offered. One of the volunteers had been in hospital the previous year and had been very pleased to receive a bouquet of flowers as soon as she let Age Concern know she was out of action. Another said that the volunteer co-ordinator "treats you like a friend, a volunteer, and doesn't make demands".

Barriers to volunteering by older people and how to overcome them

As well as identifying key factors in the successful recruitment and retention of older volunteers, the experience of the various projects funded under the Initiative also provided insights into obstacles to the involvement of older people in volunteering. Four kinds of obstacle were found:

- the policies and practices of volunteer-involving organisations

- the attitudes of older people themselves

- practical obstacles

- cultural barriers.

The first three of these were also identified in the IVR's research (IVR, 1999), while the fourth was identified in discussion with the organisers of projects which recruited older volunteers from black and minority ethnic communities.

The policies and practices of volunteer-involving organisations

The first set of obstacles to greater participation by older people in volunteering was negative stereotypes of older people and their capacities. The IVR's research suggested that organisations which involve volunteers are "infected by ageism" of which the three most common symptoms are:

- an upper age limit for volunteers

- a bias towards younger volunteers

- a failure to offer older volunteers a sufficiently wide range of activities.

The first symptom of ageism is the imposition of an upper age limit for volunteers. One justification for an age limit, as the IVR study found and this research confirmed, was the alleged difficulty of arranging insurance, especially for drivers but also for other volunteers, who were aged 70 or over. Some organisations had, however, tackled the issue and found other insurers. Overall our informants felt that many organisations were too lazy to make the effort to find another insurer or were using insurance as an excuse for discriminating against older volunteers.

Another justification was that organisations used a general age limit to deal with the difficulty of "retiring specific volunteers" who were no longer making a useful contribution to the work of the organisation or who might even have become an embarrassment to it. Informants felt that organisations found it easier to impose a retirement age for all volunteers rather than make an assessment of the individual volunteer's capacity to contribute to the work; to reshape his or her role where that was appropriate; and to explain why it was necessary that he or she might now have to retire.

The second symptom of ageism is a bias towards younger volunteers. This manifested itself in two main ways, the assumption that older volunteers were "too frail to be volunteers" and the assumption that it was "not worth training older volunteers because they will not stay with the organisation very long". Informants gave these views short shrift. Some older volunteers had health problems but many were in good health. But, in any case, projects funded under the Initiative had designed activities which enabled older and frailer people to make a valuable contribution as volunteers. Informants reported that older people generally stayed longer with an organisation than people in the younger age group and the investment in training for them thus bore dividends.

The *Inside Out* Project
This project set out to recruit volunteers from among the older people who did not see themselves as volunteers and who would not be seen by others in that light. Many of those they have involved were residents in care homes and sheltered housing or users of day centres.

The third symptom of ageism is a tendency to offer older people a narrow range of opportunities, often the least interesting and least demanding tasks. Organisations assumed that older volunteers were content with undemanding tasks like making the tea or arranging the flowers; that they preferred to be involved with other older people; and that they wanted to continue to do the things they had done in their working life. However, many of the informants in this research contradicted these views, and the projects funded under the Initiative offered a very wide range of opportunities to older volunteers.

Overall, then, overcoming ageism in volunteer-involving organisations means addressing deep-seated assumptions and rethinking established policies and procedures. Volunteers who participated in the study made it clear that the way organisations behaved was a symptom of a wider problem of negative stereotypes of older people: "When you become a certain age you're put in a certain box".

Voluntary Service Overseas (VSO) was engaged in a five-year project to recruit volunteers who were more representative of the UK population. Its project, funded under the Initiative, involved:

- tackling global disadvantage by realising older people's potential

- conducting research to establish how best to attract people who were over 50 and what the barriers to their recruitment might be

- revising VSO's recruitment procedures and literature

- organising promotional events and producing publicity materials.

VSO's project staff felt that, as a result of their work, the agency was "now more obviously inclusive" (although the staff group remained predominantly made up of younger people). There were important lessons to be learned from VSO's experience. If a major change of this kind was to be successful it required:

- getting key people "on board" at an early stage

- making sure the organisation as a whole was committed to the change; there was no use setting up an "older persons" unit when its agenda did not fit with that of the rest of the organisation

- realising that changing one aspect of the process was not enough; the whole approach needed to be rethought and redesigned

- institutionalising and embedding the changes.

Ageism occurred not only in volunteering organisations but in agencies with which projects needed to collaborate. The Inside Out project had worked hard to overcome the resistance of the staff of some residential homes, sheltered housing and day centres to the involvement of their clients as volunteers and participants in the projects. Other projects promoting intergenerational work had found "negative attitudes" among school teachers. To what extent this was a product of ageism or a "professional" prejudice against volunteers is not entirely clear. It was pointed out to us that the training of most professionals had not equipped them to work with volunteers and they could be nervous or jealous of their participation. As one project leader told us: "Volunteering empowers people but professionals do not necessarily like that"

The attitudes of older people

The second set of obstacles to greater participation by older people in volunteering was the attitudes of older people themselves. The IVR's Good Practice Guide (Dingle, 2001) highlights three ways in which older people might be discouraged from volunteering. They might:

- have other activities they preferred to devote their time to

- decide that retirement means ceasing to be involved in any activity at all

- have prejudices about being involved with some kinds of activities or client groups.

The fieldwork provided evidence of a rather more complex set of circumstances.

In many cases older people's lack of motivation seemed to stem from a lack of understanding or knowledge of what volunteering might entail. "A lot of people think it is like work" was one view; for some older people this might have been a reason for getting involved but, for others, it was the reverse. Other project staff reported that they had great difficulty getting people to understand "what volunteering was about". The stereotyped figure of the "typical volunteer" – female, white, middle class and in late middle age also tended to discourage those who did not resemble her from coming forward.

In other cases older people's apparent apathy seemed to be the result of a lack of confidence and self-belief or of health problems. Project staff and volunteers emphasised the need to help older volunteers develop confidence in their abilities and recognise the value of their experience and skills. As people became older and their health declined, their desire and ability to volunteer decreased – although the Inside Out project saw that as all the more reason to provide people with incentives to take part in volunteering and arrest the process of decline. The two sides of this perception were neatly encapsulated by the volunteer who told us that "age is a frame of mind" but, as you get older, "you do get weary".

Practical barriers

The third set of obstacles to greater participation by older people in volunteering was practical barriers of poverty and restricted mobility. Informants noted that older people who were living on low incomes would find it difficult to volunteer unless their out-of-pocket expenses were met in full. Some volunteers felt that mileage rates for car use were inadequate and, in some cases, they were not reimbursed for telephone calls, postage and stationery. Informants also stressed the importance of volunteers being paid promptly and without the embarrassment of having to ask for their expenses.

Mobility was a common problem for older people. They might have difficulty travelling for health reasons. Some did not have a car or were no longer able to drive at all or at night because of failing eyesight. Public transport, especially in rural areas, was highly unsatisfactory. Older people were less likely to travel in bad weather or to areas where they feared crime. Informants suggested three ways of addressing these problems. The first – and most common – suggestion was to provide transport for those who needed it in order to take part in volunteering. The second was to plan activities in order to minimise travel problems – for example, by organising them on a local or neighbourhood basis, so people did not have to travel far, or by arranging activities in the daytime when buses were running and at times when cheap fares were available. The third option, which required a more creative approach, was to think about what kinds of volunteering people could do without leaving their home. Here the Internet and e-mail had opened up a range of possibilities.

Dark Horse Venture: Inside Out Projects
One of the projects brought together older people and school children by e-mail. The older people developed skills in using the computer and the children learned about recent social history. The children enjoyed reading what the older people wrote and wanted to maintain contact with them. They also felt that they "understood old people better" since taking part in the project and valued them more as a group within the local community.

Cultural barriers

In addition to the barriers to volunteering which affected older people generally, there were a further set of obstacles for black and Asian elders. Informants suggested that those who might have volunteered in mainstream organisations either faced or feared racial discrimination as well as ageism. Those who might be involved in organisations based in the black or Asian communities had to overcome cultural barriers. Some cultures did not have a tradition of volunteering (although informal help was provided within the community). There could be problems about language and there were issues about caste and gender divisions. The projects for black and Asian elders tended to be small scale and based very much on face-to-face contact and the use of networks as ways of overcoming these difficulties.

Somali Women's Association and Welfare Group: *Somali Women's Education and Training* **Project**
This project worked with women who had come to Sheffield because of the civil war in Somalia. It provided an opportunity for women who felt isolated in a new country to come together in the comfort of an all-women's group made up of people with a common culture. Together they learned English, cooking, sewing, embroidery and other skills. The nine or ten older women who had been recruited as volunteers found it a new experience because there was no tradition of volunteering in Somalia. They helped with cooking, assisted the tutors, helped look after the children who came to the centre with their mothers and undertook some interpreting. There was a strong philosophy of mutual aid and the sharing of skills, and little distinction was made between the roles and statuses of "volunteers" and "users".

Recruiting older volunteers

The various projects used a variety of means of publicising opportunities and recruiting volunteers. The most popular were:

- printed materials such as leaflets, posters and bookmarks

- use of the local media – newspapers and radio

- events, displays, exhibitions and open days; the Activage project in Burnley, for example, put on an exhibition of traditional wedding clothes and garments for other special occasions. The Dark Horse Venture had its own mobile "roadshow" which toured the country.

Much of the publicity was directed to:

- places where older people were likely to be found – such as GPs' surgeries, day centres, sheltered housing and churches

- people like social workers who were likely to be in contact with older people

- groups in which potential volunteers would be already involved – including older people's forums and groups drawn from business and the professions.

Informants found that activities of this kind played a useful part in a publicity and recruitment strategy. They believed, however, that they were unlikely to succeed unless they were accompanied by vigorous efforts to make personal contact both with potential volunteers and with the staff or leaders of other organisations. They felt that successful recruitment was dependent on someone making a direct suggestion or request to the potential volunteer that he or she should become involved. In many cases the project leader or other members of staff would make contact. In others someone connected with another organisation, such as the manager of a day centre, might take the lead. One project had targeted the "movers and shakers" of the local community as its initial volunteers, confident that they would bring in other people. Project organisers also felt strongly that existing volunteers were the best recruiting agents because they brought along their friends or neighbours. Some volunteers, however, had become involved more or less by chance; one woman only joined an older people's forum because she had driven some friends to the inaugural meeting as the result of a local bus strike.

Informants also felt that successful recruitment depended on tailoring the approach to the kind of activity involved and the identity of the target group of older people. Working with an Asian community with no tradition of formal volunteering, one project leader stressed the teachings of Islam about helping others as a means of describing volunteering. She then encouraged people to stop believing they were too old or infirm to play an active role, a process she described as "more like empowering than recruiting them". At the other end of the spectrum projects recruited volunteers by offering them the training and the chance to share their interest with others.

> **Ravidassia Community Centre: *Izzat and Seva* Project**
> When the co-ordinator first came into post she had tried advertising the project through placing written publicity in places frequented by older people – the town hall, libraries, community centres, day centres, hospitals, supermarkets, etc. This took some time to organise because of problems getting leaflets translated into the relevant languages. Her approach was to target different areas on different days, wait a couple of weeks and then, if she had not had a response, go back and try to speak to the managers. This produced little response, but when she began to arrange to speak directly to older people, she found that they were interested. She talked about the benefits of volunteering, asked people about their interests, and invited them to open days at the centre where they were offered food and shown videos.

Informants pointed to some more general lessons about the way to approach publicity and recruitment. Several projects had adopted a "volunteer-centred" approach. Instead of trying to fit older people into an existing process – "here are the opportunities and here is what you can do" – they began by discussing the individual's skills, experiences and aspirations. One project found that its energetic programme of talking to groups with older people as members about the ways they could be involved in their work produced very few volunteers. When they changed course, however, and spent more time listening to what older people were interested in doing, the volunteers came forward. Another project leader felt that approaches to older people should follow the model of the Millennium Volunteers[4] programme whose theme was "build on what you're into". Another project worker using a community development approach spent time promoting a discussion about what needed to be done on a disadvantaged housing estate before encouraging people to decide what they were going to do.

Volunteers and project staff also felt that there was a more general message that needed to be promoted; one of them expressed this as the need to get across that volunteering was about "more than helping in a hospital or a charity shop". Publicity needed to inform people about the range of activities volunteers were involved in and to give them clear examples of what they could do. These messages, it was agreed, needed to be delivered to older people themselves but also to the people who were in regular contact with them.

Some of the informants offered some thoughts about the messenger rather than the message. Successful encouragement and promotion of volunteering by older people depends on the ambassadorial efforts of project staff and existing volunteers. One striking feature of the data collected was the enthusiasm with which they went about spreading the word about the benefits of volunteering by older people and overcoming the obstacles they encountered.

Selection, induction, training and support of older volunteers

Selection

The policies and procedures adopted by the various projects funded under the Initiative varied considerably as they chose approaches which were appropriate to the purpose of each project and the activities which volunteers were expected to undertake.

---

4.   A Department for Education and Skills initiative aimed at encouraging more 16–24 year olds to volunteer their time for the benefit of others.

For some projects, selection was not an issue. The primary purpose of the Dark Horse Ventures' *Inside Out* project was to provide opportunities for older people to participate in voluntary activity, and all who were interested in taking part were welcome. Similarly, Help the Aged's *Speaking Up for Our Age* forums accepted as members anybody who shared their aims.

Other projects carried out their selection processes in a fairly informal fashion. This emphasis on informality was associated with a view that older volunteers often lacked confidence and needed to be encouraged to believe they had a useful role to play. In some cases the informality was the result of prior knowledge; Manufacturing Science and Finance (MSF) volunteers had been active in other roles in the union, while one of the *Activage* workers did not take up references for people in the community she already knew – they would have found this odd. The leader of Ravidassia Community Centre's *Izzat and Seva* project had simplified its procedure; she visited potential volunteers in their own homes and helped them complete a very simple application form on the spot. The great majority of projects interviewed prospective volunteers, but they saw this as an informal discussion of their mutual expectations or "more a chat about getting to know each other" than an exercise in selection.

There were, however, a number of projects for which organisations operated formal and fairly rigorous procedures in order to protect the interests of vulnerable users. These included the projects which worked with young people (The Children's Society's Advocates for Children and Young People Project; NACRO's Golden Years Activities Units projects; and RSVP's *Better Government for Older People* projects that worked in schools) and the befriending project for older people with dementia run by the Alzheimer's Society. The volunteers met during the research were generally happy to go through these more rigorous selection processes; they felt that they were appropriate and necessary for the activities in which they were to be involved.

Age Concern England: Activage

Most volunteers came through contact with friends and families. The co-ordinator met everyone individually and talked about what volunteering involved, including the need to be committed and reliable, and asked people about their motivation and any previous experience. He/she asked people for the name of two referees and suggested that they observe sessions taking place before committing themselves.

Another approach, used by *Pabulum's Lifetimes* project, offered anybody who was interested the opportunity to join an initial training course and, in effect, used the training as a means of selecting volunteers. The volunteers met were divided in their views about the advantages and disadvantages of this method. While they thought it valuable that people should have an extended opportunity to discover whether or not they were interested in and committed to the activities of the project, they also felt that the time and efforts of the organisers had been wasted on those who did not became volunteers.

Induction

Most projects used informal methods of induction. Informants stated that most project organisers were "generally quite careful and thorough" in providing new volunteers with background information about the project and organisation (sometimes with an emphasis on health and safety issues). They suggested that it was important to give volunteers clear information about what was expected of them and how this would help the project to meet its aims. They regarded it as good practice to provide the volunteers with a pack of written material. However, some volunteers were dissatisfied with their induction: they regretted that they had not been given a clear statement of what was expected, had not been informed about the organisation with which they were involved and had not been introduced to other volunteers. Some of them felt disadvantaged as a result.

Induction took different forms. For some projects it was part and parcel of the initial training rather than a separate process. In others new volunteers worked alongside the project leader or a more experienced volunteer until they felt confident enough to take responsibility for their own activities. Even where there was quite extensive initial training, project staff still found it necessary to "hold people's hands" until they gained confidence.

Support

Most projects explicitly addressed the need to provide appropriate levels of support to older people. In some cases this meant providing more support or support over a longer period than was usual in the organisation. This involved:

- a combination of individual support and group meetings

- treating older volunteers as individuals with different needs, worries and aspirations rather than as an homogeneous group

- employing staff who were accessible and supportive – who treated you "as a friend"

- promoting positive relationships between volunteers through regular meetings and, where numbers permitted, allocating volunteers to a small mutual support group led by an experienced volunteer.

(Such support, however, ought to be good practice for all volunteers, rather than an 'extra' for older volunteers).

Dark Horse Venture: *Inside Out* **Project**

Staff were aware that many of the people they worked with needed a lot of support if they were to complete their chosen activity. One way of providing support was through a mentor chosen by the older person themselves – this could be a friend or a sheltered housing warden who could take an interest and confirm when the activity had been completed. Staff also telephoned to check if there was anything the volunteer wanted to discuss.

Training

Most projects provided new recruits with initial training – which volunteers generally found useful and adequate – and also offered opportunities for further training at a later stage. The dangers of generalising about such a heterogeneous group as people of 50 and over was illustrated by differences in informants' attitudes to training. Some volunteers felt that accreditation of their training was an important additional incentive for involvement, while others found the additional paperwork associated with a qualification irksome and unnecessary: "That's for younger people".

Organising the activities of older volunteers

There was widespread agreement among informants that volunteering should be "well organised". Most of the volunteers who took part in the study – and the project staff – had much to praise and little to criticise about the projects with which they were involved. The evidence of those who did have serious criticisms is particularly helpful in identifying what good practice should be by pointing to shortcomings and failures.

In the first place they identified shortcomings in the design and planning of activities, notably:

- inability to plan "properly" how the project would operate

- failure to ensure that the necessary equipment and materials were available

- inadequate support by paid staff for volunteers

- timescales and targets which were unlikely or impossible to achieve.

Secondly, they pointed to problems in implementing projects, including:

- failure to provide volunteers with something to do immediately after they had finished their training

- failure to ensure that volunteers had enough to do at any time or to explain the reasons for the lack of activity (such as diminishing referrals from statutory agencies).

Finally they highlighted underlying problems which stemmed from project organisers' negative attitudes towards older people as volunteers, specifically:

- a tendency to stereotype roles as suitable or unsuitable for older volunteers

- a failure to value volunteers.

The importance of avoiding these shortcomings was emphasised by informants' views that older volunteers were more likely than their younger counterparts to complain or vote with their feet if their activities were poorly organised.

In general, informants agreed that an effective organisational framework for the involvement of older volunteers required three key elements. These were:

- adequate planning

- appropriate policies and systems

- enthusiastic and committed volunteer co-ordinators with organisational and "people management" skills.

Volunteers and project staff suggested that policies and systems needed to be designed to strike a balance between two needs. On the one hand, they needed to be informal and flexible enough to enable volunteers to create their roles and develop their individual contributions to the project. On the other, they needed to provide formal and regular ways in which activities could be monitored and controlled.

Project development and organisational arrangements to support volunteering by older people

Creating and maintaining greater opportunities for volunteering by older people also required projects to address wider organisational issues. Four key themes were highlighted by informants:

- the need for organisational commitment

- the importance of partnership with other bodies

- the assessment of need

- the need to be realistic about size and timescale.

Organisational commitment

Organisations made different levels of commitment to projects, and the greater the commitment, the greater the likelihood of the project's success. Key elements in treating the project as a "corporate venture" included:

- the appointment of experienced project staff (at an appropriate level of pay). This was not only a practical consideration but an indication of strategic commitment

- integration of the project into the work of the organisation. One major project experienced serious difficulties and delays in its earlier days because the senior management of the large national organisation concerned had not taken their ownership of the project seriously enough. Senior managers had not "paved the way" for the arrival of the volunteer co-ordinator by ensuring that the key people whose collaboration would be needed at the operational level were well briefed about the project

- clear vision of what the project was to do and how it was to fit into the work of the organisation. One local project organiser had no support from anyone who knew the area and its problems. Volunteers in another local project had very different ideas about its agenda and role than staff in the organisation's headquarters.

Voluntary Service Overseas: Tackling global disadvantage by realising older people's potential

VSO initiated a radical revision of its recruitment in order to achieve a more demographically balanced mix of volunteers. In order to ensure that the changes were more than cosmetic, it identified not only what needed to be done but who were the key people who could make it happen. It believed that once these people came on board, the desired changes would be "institutionalised".

Partnership with other bodies

Many of the projects were developed with a variety of organisational partners. However, in order to reap the benefits of working with partners, organisations had to make a substantial investment of time and resources. Key to this was a need to:

- be clear about the aims of the project

- be clear about working arrangements.

The Dark Horse Venture: *Inside Out* Project

This project had mixed success in gaining access to potential volunteers in partnership with day centres and sheltered housing. Some day centre and scheme managers used their position as gatekeepers to act as a barrier, but those who could be persuaded of the value of the Inside Out project became invaluable allies. A member of staff in one of the day centres played a key role as the access point or gatekeeper for the project and was very popular with the users. They felt very strongly that he "always got ideas that people can do and encourages us to do them".

Assessment of need

Another key factor in designing and developing a successful project was to base it on adequate information. The projects were aware of the need for their activities (and the feasibility of undertaking them successfully) from a variety of sources.

Many of the projects took the form of extensions to, or the enhancement of, existing activities. Here the need had already been clearly established or a demand had been articulated by those who would benefit from the new service either directly or indirectly (as in the case of schools, residential care homes and day centres).

Some projects were based on a general appreciation of the circumstances which prevented some older people from volunteering. *The Dark Horse Venture's* involvement had been prompted by an understanding born of long experience that many older people either were not motivated to volunteer or faced major obstacles to their involvement. There was a need to address this issue and "take their thoughts out, lift their minds and broaden their horizons".

Other projects grew out of reviews by organisations of the demographic profile of their current volunteers. This had led, among others, to the projects run by NAVB and *The National Trust* which aimed to change the profile so that it reflected more accurately the diversity of the population at large.

Finally, some projects were the product of research into the needs of potential users and the feasibility of meeting them. Help the Aged's Rural Initiative was based on earlier studies and included a process of needs assessment as the starting point of its activities.

Realism about the size and timescale of projects

Many informants were concerned about the tendency of organisations to develop projects with unrealistic timescales and over-ambitious aims. They identified a number of issues for good practice in project development among which the following were seen to provide important lessons:

- Projects needed a realistic timescale. Funding for all of the projects was short-term and for some of them it was very short term indeed. In a number of cases the aims of the project were disproportionate to the amount of time available.

- Many projects required a long-term strategy. Inflexible timescales and tight deadlines meant that little or no time could be devoted to laying solid foundations when the pressure was for "quick results". In many instances, little thought was given to how the initial short-term project might be followed through.

- Projects needed realistic levels of resourcing. The mismatch of project objectives and the time available for achieving them was in some cases matched by a similar failure to acknowledge and provide an adequate level of resources.

In some cases over-ambitious aims were revised and scaled down, but other projects achieved comparatively little in concrete terms.

These problems were exacerbated by a number of practical difficulties which included:

- the time it took for many projects to complete the formalities of negotiating contracts so that funds could be released. In many cases this delayed the start of the project and had a knock-on effect on the planning and implementation of its activities

- further delays caused by the time it took to recruit staff. This process could only begin when the funding had been confirmed and, even if it was a fairly straightforward process, a further delay was inevitable

- in some projects, the loss of members of staff. The inflexibility of the programme and its short-term nature could mean that the loss of momentum when a member of staff left and had to be replaced could have a major impact on the work.

4   Conclusions

The direct impact on older people and volunteering

What did the Initiative achieve? It clearly demonstrated that older people could be successfully recruited and involved as volunteers in a variety of roles and settings.

The limitations of the data recorded by the individual projects mean that it is difficult to provide a detailed statistical breakdown about the characteristics of the older people who became directly involved in volunteering activity as a result of the Initiative. But it can be reported with some confidence that they included:

- people who had not previously been involved in volunteering and people who were undertaking volunteer roles and tasks that were significantly different from the kinds of activities they had undertaken in the past

- people from across the wide spectrum of ages – from their 50s to their 80s

- people from lower socio-economic groups as well as the middle class people who are heavily represented among the volunteering population at large

- people from black and minority ethnic communities

- men as well as women.

Older volunteers took part in a variety of activities, played a variety of roles and were involved in a range of settings. While the majority of the projects funded under the Initiative which directly recruited older people as volunteers operated a service model of volunteering, others took approaches based on *self-help, community development or participation* and one involved *campaigning* activities.

Across the projects older volunteers were involved in a wide range of activities:

- direct work with users

- support roles

- practical tasks

- leadership and managerial activities.

Across the projects, too, the activities of older volunteers helped a variety of users or beneficiaries. While many projects addressed the needs of people of all age groups, some of them focused on the needs of two specific groups of users:

- other older people (including isolated and frail older people and elders in black and ethnic minority communities)

- children and young people (including young people at risk and school children).

This body of evidence thus:

- supports an underlying assumption of the Initiative that older people from a variety of backgrounds could be attracted into volunteering if greater efforts were made to recruit them

- suggests that older volunteers could play a part in a wider range of activities than is usually expected of them.

The extent to which individual projects were able to recruit and involve older volunteers varied considerably. Explaining these variations is not a simple matter, but it is possible to offer some tentative propositions which would repay further investigation:

- Organisations whose mission or purpose is to promote the well-being of older people have a considerable advantage in involving older people as volunteers. Their understanding of the needs and aspirations of older people and their access to existing networks mean that they can engage with older people, develop effective methods of recruitment and deploy older volunteers in appropriate roles speedily and effectively.

- The extent to which volunteering is a recognised and central feature of an organisation's work is another factor in its ability to recruit older volunteers quickly and effectively. Those for which volunteering is not so central need time to promote volunteering as an activity and develop appropriate ways of supporting volunteers as well as to come to terms with the needs and aspirations of older people.

- Older people from black and minority ethnic communities with little or no tradition of formal volunteering are more likely to volunteer within their own communities than in "mainstream" organisations. Small-scale projects with a mutual aid ethos offer a valuable means of transition from informal helping to more formal volunteering.

- The contribution of older people is likely to be especially valuable in providing education and recreational activities for frail and isolated older people; intergenerational activities with school-age children and helping other people with long-term health problems to manage their condition.

Other ways of promoting volunteering by older people

The Initiative went beyond the direct recruitment and involvement of older people as volunteers. It also aimed to identify and disseminate good practice and generally to promote the idea of volunteering by older people.

Guidance about "good practice" was developed in the following areas:

- identifying and overcoming barriers to volunteering by older people. This was addressed to voluntary organisations which involve volunteers in their work

- support for volunteering by older and retired employees of local government

- encouraging volunteering by black and minority ethnic older people

- mentoring.

Vigorous attempts were made to disseminate the guidance distilled from this experience within the period for which the work was funded, but there is little evidence that the work will be followed up over a longer timescale. As a result the impact of some well-executed and important work may well be limited.

The same conclusion could be drawn about the projects which concentrated on generally promoting volunteering by older people. The photographic exhibition celebrating older people as active members of the community had an impact on those who used it in conjunction with other activities to promote the participation of older people in volunteering.

These appeared to be, however, one-off events rather than part of a continuing process. Similarly the modest efforts of the Northampton Volunteer Bureau succeeded in raising the profile of older people as potential volunteers with local organisations, but there is no evidence of any concrete ways in which they made an impact at the time – let alone in the longer run.

Specific aims of the original working group

The review of the achievements of the Initiative drawn together in the first two sections of this part of the report provides an account of the extent to which three of the specific objectives originally identified by the Older Volunteers Initiative Group have been met.

Much of the programme involved successful activities which addressed two fairly broad aims set by the Group:

- to ensure that volunteering opportunities are brought to the attention of older people in a way that encourages them to take part

- to promote volunteering opportunities by focusing on community issues where voluntary activity has a clear role.

Projects have developed a variety of ways of bringing opportunities for volunteering to the attention of older people and presenting them in a way that makes it more likely that they will respond to the invitation.

They have also created and maintained opportunities for volunteering by older people which address a range of community needs which can be met appropriately and effectively through voluntary action.

A third – rather more specific – objective was to remove barriers to the recruitment of older volunteers.

Many of the projects were successful demonstrations of how to overcome practical barriers to volunteering by older people. These activities were complemented by the work of the IVR discussed above (IVR, 1999). The lessons to be learned from these experiences are discussed below and some of the implications for the recommendations are spelt out. The Initiative thus removed some barriers for some people and identified ways of tackling those that remain.

The fourth objective was more specific still, to increase the commitment to employee and retiree volunteering.

The Initiative has moved this agenda forward in three ways. The NCV's *MAVERIC* project has set out guidelines for good practice in employee and retiree volunteering in local authorities, and a number of authorities are developing policies and practices in line with these. BiTC's *Time to Volunteer* project has forged links between companies and local voluntary and community sector organisations in one area and hopes to replicate this in other parts of the country. Finally, the NT's *Supporting and Developing Opportunities for Older Volunteers* project has developed a pack of materials setting out the opportunities for volunteering within the organisation and beyond which will be used by people running pre-retirement programmes. The Initiative has thus identified methods of developing a greater commitment to employee and retiree volunteering. They remain, however, largely potential rather than actual means of securing greater commitment to volunteering in this context.

Learning the lessons

Important lessons have been learnt about encouraging and promoting volunteering by older people from the diverse range of activities funded under the Initiative.

Older people as volunteers

- Older people bring valuable qualities and skills to volunteering that are rarely possessed by younger people. These include "life skills", maturity, authority, tolerance, commitment and self-confidence.

- Like other volunteers older people are motivated by a number of factors. Volunteering enables them to meet personal needs and interests and provides them with opportunities for personal development. For obvious reasons older people are unlikely to be motivated by the need to improve their employment prospects. They tend to volunteer in order to feel useful, valuable and wanted and to "put something back" into the community. Some have a specific interest in the welfare of other older people. Older volunteers are often prompted to become involved to "fill the gap" left by retirement or bereavement.

- Older volunteers remain committed provided they are kept busy and feel that what they are doing is useful or valuable. Many of them also want the opportunity to create their individual contribution to the organisation and to take part in its decision-making. Opportunities for personal development and social interaction are also important factors in ensuring that older volunteers are retained.

- Older volunteers have other commitments and organisations need to recognise the claims on them from their families and their entitlement to holidays.

- All volunteers need to feel valued but this is especially important for many older volunteers who lack confidence in the value of their experience and skills.

Barriers to volunteering and how to overcome them

- The policies and practices of organisations which involve volunteers in their activities can present obstacles to the involvement of older people. These might include an upper age limit for volunteers, a bias towards younger volunteers and a failure to offer older volunteers a sufficiently wide range of voluntary activity. These are symptomatic of a wider problem of negative stereotypes of older people. Changing these attitudes requires a commitment by the organisation as a whole to the process.

- The attitudes of older people themselves may act as barriers to involvement. Lack of interest may be due to ignorance or lack of understanding of what volunteering might entail or to a lack of self-confidence.

- Lack of money and problems with transport may make it difficult for older people to volunteer. Many older people are on low incomes and it is essential that they should receive adequate out-of-pocket expenses and that these should be paid promptly and as a matter of course. Another common problem is mobility; transport should be provided for those who need it; activities can be planned to minimise travel problems; and people can undertake volunteer activity without leaving home.

- Cultural differences may make it difficult for elders from black and minority ethnic communities to volunteer, especially where there is no tradition of formal volunteering. These can be overcome by small-scale projects with strong elements of mutual aid where there is sensitive face-to-face contact by project staff with potential volunteers.

Publicity and recruitment

- While a wide range of methods may be used to advertise opportunities for volunteering, these need to be used in conjunction with vigorous efforts to make personal contact with potential volunteers.

- The approach should involve listening to what older people are interested in doing and building on the individual's skills and experience rather than fitting people into preconceived roles.

- Older people need to be told about the whole range of volunteering opportunities.

- Existing volunteers and project staff are the best people to "sell" volunteering to older people.

Selection, induction, training and support

- Selection procedures should be designed in the light of the activity involved. Where volunteers are involved with children or vulnerable people, rigorous screening is appropriate, while selection for many other activities need not be very formal. "Interviews" can be an informal discussion of mutual expectations. Informality of this kind can help to encourage older people who lack confidence to take part.

- All new volunteers need to be given clear information about what is expected of them and what they can expect in terms of support. Older volunteers may need more and longer support in the early stages than younger people. This can be provided through individual supervision and group meetings.

- Older volunteers tend to value opportunities for training but opinions about accreditation are sharply divided.

Organising the activities of volunteers

- Older volunteers are likely to complain or leave if their activities are poorly organised.

- An effective organisational framework will involve adequate planning, appropriate policies and systems and, above all, volunteer co-ordinators who are enthusiastic and committed as well as having organisational and people management skills.

Wider organisational arrangements

- Organisations aiming to recruit and involve older people as volunteers need to commit the whole of the organisation to this purpose; this involves support from senior management; the articulation of a clear vision of the Initiative's purpose and rationale; and the commitment of adequate resources.

- Working in partnership with other agencies can be the key to success and sustainability, but it is also an extremely challenging task.

- Successful projects are based on an adequate assessment of community needs and the feasibility of the proposed response.

- The design of activities aimed at promoting volunteering by older people needs to be based on realistic assessments of the resources required and the timescale needed to accomplish goals.

Limitations of the approach used by the Initiative

The Initiative has thus achieved a great deal. It has made possible a range of projects which have provided a variety of older people with diverse opportunities to engage in volunteering. In the process it has made a contribution to meeting a considerable number of community needs. It has enabled projects to identify and disseminate advice about good practice in the recruitment and deployment of volunteers. It has also made possible the development of ways of promoting volunteering by older people and advanced the knowledge of opportunities for volunteering by older people. Finally, it has provided lessons which can help to develop more opportunities in the future on which recommendations to the various interested parties can be based.

This can be seen as a considerable body of achievement. At the same time the design and implementation of the Initiative had serious limitations which reduced its capacity to meet its overall aim of encouraging volunteering by older people.

The fundamental difficulty was the decision to cast the Initiative in the form of a funding programme rather than a strategy. This was essentially a reactive rather than a proactive approach in which the programme was formed by aggregating the result of the bids for funding made by different organisations with different interests and different agendas. This approach had its advantages: it encouraged organisations to put forward a range of innovative and creative proposals. But it also had disadvantages: it was not clearly designed and systematically developed to meet a coherent series of aims and objectives:

- there were a number of small-scale and short-term projects which, in the longer term, contributed little to the impact of the programme

- the focus on achieving targets, many of which were unrealistic may well have undermined the projects' capacity to lay strong foundations for future work

- the aggregate nature of the programme did not allow for collaborative working and the sharing of information among the projects, which means that projects were not fully able to take advantage of research and the compilation of good practice.

Recommendations

Recommendations for organisations which involve volunteers

In putting forward these recommendations for action by organisations which involve – or intend to involve – older volunteers in their work, it is important to be conscious of the heterogeneity of the organisations concerned and the diversity of the contexts within which they operate. In particular it is worth noting the distinctions between:

- organisations which exist to promote the welfare of older people, which have an understanding of older people's qualities and aspirations but may need to develop their ability to involve volunteers

- organisations which are experienced in their involvement of volunteers but have limited expertise in dealing with older people

- organisations which lack experience of involving volunteers and expertise in dealing with older people.

For the sake of simplicity, however, a generic set of recommendations has been produced.

Vision and commitment

Before engaging in detailed planning for the involvement of older people as volunteers, organisations need to give serious attention to three areas. They should:

- develop and articulate a clear and coherent vision of the rationale for involving older volunteers in the work of the organisation which identifies the expected benefits to the organisation and to the volunteers

- secure the commitment of the organisation as a whole to the work necessary to ensure that older volunteers are successfully involved in its activities. This means gaining the informed and explicit support of the governing body, the senior management team and those at operational level whose work will be affected by the involvement of older volunteers

- consult the people outside the organisation whose co-operation and collaboration will be necessary if older people are to be involved in its work; these may include staff of other voluntary organisations or statutory agencies with which it works.

Planning

Having laid the foundations for the successful involvement of older people in its work, the organisation needs to develop concrete plans for a project or programme of activities. This involves:

- conducting an assessment of the needs which the proposed activities will address

- undertaking a feasibility study in order to be clear how and to what extent the proposed programme or project can address the needs that have been identified

- identifying the resources required to support the activities. These may include the appointment of dedicated staff to act as volunteer managers or co-ordinators; the time commitment needed from existing staff; and the provision of transport, out-of-pocket expenses, premises, equipment and running costs

- developing the structures and systems needed to support volunteering by older people. This may involve ensuring that volunteer managers or co-ordinators have appropriate levels of responsibility and authority and that they are given a clear role within the managerial structure of the organisation. It will also mean putting in place systems for recruitment, induction, training and support before volunteers are recruited

- setting out a realistic timescale for the establishment of the programme or project, bearing in mind the time needed for staff recruitment and induction and for establishing the necessary structure and systems

- exploring the ways in which the work can be sustained in the long run and beyond short term project funding.

Implementation

At the operational level it is suggested that organisations should be aware that:

- effective recruitment of older volunteers depends heavily on personal contact and the use of social networks

- successful contact with potential volunteers involves listening to what they are interested in doing and letting them know about the full range of possible volunteer roles open to them

- opportunities for volunteering by older people need to be flexible to take account of other commitments and open-ended to the extent that the volunteer can shape his or her role rather than simply slot into preconceived roles

- selection, induction and training should be appropriate to the role and context of the volunteering activity. Any volunteer is entitled to a clear discussion about the expectations of both parties and, where necessary, volunteers will have to be "vetted". But these procedures can be informal. Older volunteers may need more support than younger people and this should be planned for. Training is often valued by older volunteers but there are mixed views on accreditation

- opportunities for volunteering should be as diverse as possible and not constrained by preconceptions of "appropriate" tasks for older volunteers. Organisations should be imaginative about the ways in which they are involved

- attention should be given to overcoming the barriers to volunteering by older people. As well as practical issues like mobility and spending power these may include a lack of confidence on the part of the older volunteer or bias towards younger people within the organisation

- older volunteers are a valuable resource. Every effort should be made to ensure that their activities are well organised and that they and the experience and skills they bring to the organisation are recognised and valued.

Recommendations for government

There is a clear need for the promotion of volunteering by older people to be undertaken not as a "one-off" or on a project-by-project basis but as a continuing activity. This should involve a twin-track approach. In the first place volunteering should take its place within a cross-departmental strategy of encouraging and promoting the idea of older people as healthy, fit, alert and active members of the community. Secondly, volunteering by older people should be actively promoted at national and local level (and this is the agenda of the newly established Experience Corps).

There is a case for strategic funding and support for two kinds of activity which projects funded under the Initiative undertook and which need to be built on over a longer period of time if they are to deliver substantial rewards. These are:

- *Volunteering by employees and former employees* – there is an opportunity to make a significant impact in this area by following through on the work of projects in promoting good practice by local authority employers; using the Business in the Community model of bringing together companies and their local voluntary sector to identify opportunities for employee volunteering; and developing ways of ensuring that the range of volunteering options are highlighted in programmes of preparation for retirement.

- *Promoting good practice in volunteer-involving organisations* – the recommendations listed above have been distilled from the range of experience across the projects. They – and the IVR's Good Practice Guide (Dingle, 2001) – need to be disseminated and promoted if they are to make an impact on the ways in which organisations behave and on the quantity and quality of volunteering opportunities for older people. A long term programme of events, consultancies and publications is needed to drive this forward.

As well as following up on Initiatives and learning which has taken place across the voluntary and community sector as a whole, it is recommended that the Home Office should identify ways in which they can work with other government departments and agencies to promote volunteering by older people in specific areas of policy and provision. There are three important areas which would be worth pursuing. These are:

- older volunteers as providers of services to other older people – including those who are isolated or frail. This ought to be of interest to the Department of Health

- intergenerational volunteering and especially the involvement of older volunteers with schools. This should be of interest to the Department for Education and Skills

- older volunteers as participants or leaders in developing active communities and neighbourhood renewal which should be of interest to a number of departments and agencies.

This is not an exhaustive list; other areas for consideration include:

- older volunteers and the environment

- older volunteers and cultural and heritage issues.

The final set of lessons for the Home Office are about its role as funder. In the light of the experience of the Initiative it is suggested that future funding programmes should take account of the following recommendations:

- the goals and objectives of the programme should be clear and explicit in order to facilitate the monitoring and evaluation of success

- the funders should be more proactive and work in partnership with appropriate organisations to develop activities which individually meet specific objectives of the programme and collectively enable its overall aims to be met

- the funders should ensure that the projects it funds are realistic in terms of the resources and timescale required.

Recommendations for the private sector

Companies in the private, for-profit sector have an important role to play in promoting and encouraging volunteering by older people.

It is therefore recommended that:

- companies should be encouraged to develop a strategy and a code of good practice for older volunteers

- they should seek the active support of national and local intermediary bodies and development agencies in developing this strategy

- they should forge relationships with their local voluntary sectors in order to facilitate the implementation of their strategy

- they should look to organisations like Business in the Community, local volunteer bureaux and councils for voluntary service to enable them to make and sustain links with local voluntary agencies interested in providing opportunities for older people to take part in volunteering.

Appendix 1: Summary details of all HOOVI projects

Organisation and project name	Summary of activities	Contribution to HOOVI aims	Geographical scope	Dates in operation	Amount funded
1. Age Concern England *Activage (Black and Ethnic Elders Healthy Ageing Project)*	recruit older volunteers from Asian communities to act as senior health mentors for other elders	create opportunities recruit volunteers	Burnley Nelson	07/99 to 03/01	£64,000
2. Age Concern England *Age Resource*	recruit 50-to-65 year old volunteers to introduce isolated older people to the Internet and other IT applications	create opportunities recruit volunteers	Cornwall Gateshead East Sussex Lancashire Leicestershire	07/99 to 03/00	£60,000
3. Alzheimers Disease Society (Brighton Area Branch) *Volunteer Befriending Scheme*	recruit older volunteers to befriend people with dementia living in residential care homes	create opportunities recruit volunteers	Brighton	09/99 to 06/01	£25,000
4. Arthritis Care (with Coventry University) *Older Volunteers Challenging Arthritis*	conduct research project on benefits of scheme	advance knowledge disseminate good practice	England	09/99 to 07/00	£58,000
5. Business in the Community *Time to Volunteer*	increase volunteering by olde people and especially those retiring from the business community	promote volunteering	South East Region	10/99 to 10/00	£56,000

Organisation and project name	Summary of activities	Contribution to HOOVI aims	Geographical scope	Dates in operation	Amount funded
6. The Children's Society *Advocates for Children and Young People*	recruit volunteers as advocates for young people	create opportunities recruit volunteers	Torbay	06/99 to 07/02	£54,000
7. Dark Horse Venture *Inside Out Project*	identify needs for volunteers through contact with other organisations encourage normally excluded older people to meet the need	create opportunities recruit volunteers	England	04/99 to 03/01	£50,000
8. Help the Aged *Rural Initiative*	involve older people in disadvantaged rural communities by developing and supporting projects	create opportunities recruit volunteers	Northumberland Lake District North Norfolk Wensleydale and Swaledale North Cornwall	11/00 to 03/03	£79,000
9. Help the Aged *Speaking Up for Our Age*	promote older people's forums by developing new and supporting existing forums good practice guide	create opportunities recruit volunteers disseminate good practice	England	04/99 to 03/01	£73,000
10. MSF Union *Trades Unions in the Community*	recruit and train retired union members to provide mentoring, representation and advice to voluntary organisations	create opportunities recruit volunteers	South East England Manchester Liverpool Scotland	09/99 to 03/02	£145,000

Organisation and project name	Summary of activities	Contribution to HOOVI aims	Geographical scope	Dates in operation	Amount funded
11. National Association for the Care and Resettlement of Offenders (NACRO) *Golden Year Activities Unit*	recruit older volunteers to do group work with young people and divert them from crime (Art/health project and video project)	create opportunities recruit volunteers	Walsall	09/99 to 03/02	£85,000
12. National Association of Volunteer Bureaux *Increasing the Involvement of Black Elders*	increase involvement of black elders in mainstream voluntary and community activity	recruit volunteers disseminate good practice	Birmingham Cambridge Leicester Liverpool Tower Hamlets West Wiltshire Wigan and Leigh	04/99 to 12/00	£53,000
13. Institute for Volunteering Research *Research into barriers to volunteering by older people*	conduct research on barriers to volunteering by older people disseminate good practice guide	advance knowledge disseminate good practice	England	04/99 to 03/01	£21,000
14. National Centre for Volunteering *Mature Volunteers Enriching Resources in the Community Project (MAVERIC)*	encourage local authorities to promote volunteering by older staff	advance knowledge promote volunteering disseminate good practice	England and Wales	04/99 to 03/01	£4,000

Organisation and project name	Summary of activities	Contribution to HOOVI aims	Geographical scope	Dates in operation	Amount funded
15. National Mentoring Network *Mapping of Mentoring Across Government Departments*	carry out mapping exercise in government departments	advance knowledge	England	10/98 to 04/99	£11,000
16. National Mentoring Network *Audit of Intergenerational Mentoring*	carry out audit of National Mentoring Network members	advance knowledge disseminate good practice	England	12/98 to 03/00	£5,000
17. National Trust *Supporting and Developing Opportunities for Older Volunteers*	work with local properties and local associations to develop volunteering by older people produce promotional pack for people about to retire	create opportunities promote volunteering recruit volunteers	England, Wales and Northern Ireland	01/00 to 12/03	£83,000
18. Northampton Volunteer Bureau *Year of the Older Volunteer*	production of booklets and posters	promote volunteering	Northampton	04/99 to 10/99	£600
19. Pabulum *Lifetimes*	recruit older volunteers to tackle social exclusion of frail older people in isolated rural areas	create opportunities recruit volunteers	Norfolk	04/99 to 03/02	£70,000

Organisation and project name	Summary of activities	Contribution to HOOVI aims	Geographical scope	Dates in operation	Amount funded
20. Ravidassia Community Centre *Izzat and Seva ("respect and volunteering")*	recruit older volunteers from ethnic minorities to act as mentors on health issues and befriend isolated and elderly people	create opportunities recruit volunteers	Hitchin	04/99 to 03/02	£80,000
21. and 22. Retired and Senior Volunteer Programme (RSVP) *Leaders Gathering and European Network of Older Volunteers Conference*	organise meeting of RSVP volunteers and staff produce conference pack for European Network conference	disseminate good practice	England Europe	01/99 to 09/99	£10,000 and £1,000
23. Retired and Senior Volunteers Programme *Better Government for Older People Project*	facilitate the health and well-being of older people by using the government's BGOP initiative as a vehicle for encouraging volunteering by older people	create opportunities recruit volunteers	Coventry Hackney Hartlepool Middlesborough North Yorkshire Sheffield Solihull Warwick Watford Waverley	05/99 to 03/01	£268,000

Organisation and project name	Summary of activities	Contribution to HOOVI aims	Geographical scope	Dates in operation	Amount funded
24. Somali Women's Association and Welfare Group *Somali Women's Education and Training Project*	involve volunteers in increasing the skills, confidence and ability to play an active part in the wider community	create opportunities recruit volunteers	Sheffield	04/00 to 03/01	£11,000
25. UK Secretariat for the International Year of Older Persons c/o Age Concern *England Photography Exhibition, Competition and Calendar*	organise travelling photographic exhibition and photographic competition produce and distribute calendar	promote volunteering	United Kingdom	04/99 to 03/00	£50,000
26. Voluntary Service Overseas *Tackling Global Disadvantage by Realising Older People's Potential*	match the demand from overseas partners for experienced, mature and skilled older volunteers	recruit volunteers	England	04/99 to 03/00	£43,000

References

Dingle, A. (2001) *Involving Older Volunteers: A good practice guide* London, Institute for Volunteering Research

Drury, C. (1999) *A Map of Mentoring in Three Government Departments* Wareside, Herts, Catherine Drury Associates

Hainsworth, J. and J. Barlow (2000) *Challenging Arthritis: Older Volunteers Initiative Final Report* Coventry, Coventry University

Home Office (1999) *The Older Volunteers Initiative* Mimeo

Institute for Volunteering Research (1999) *Age Discrimination and Volunteering* London, IVR

National Association of Volunteer Bureaux (2000) *Guidelines for Increasing the Involvement of Black Elders in Mainstream Volunteering* Sheffield, NAVB

National Centre for Volunteering (2000) *A good practice guide for local authorities* London, NCV

National Mentoring Network (1999) *Intergenerational Survey and Good Practice Paper* Mimeo

O'Brien, M. (1999) Speech at the launch of the Home Office Older Volunteers Initiative, London, Home Office

RDS Publications

Requests for Publications

Copies of our publications and a list of those currently available may be obtained from:

> Home Office
> Research, Development and Statistics Directorate
> Communication Development Unit
> Room 275, Home Office
> 50 Queen Anne's Gate
> London SW1H 9AT
> Telephone: 020 7273 2084 (answerphone outside of office hours)
> Facsimile: 020 7222 0211
> E-mail: publications.rds@homeoffice.gsi.gov.uk

alternatively

why not visit the RDS website at

> Internet: http://www.homeoffice.gov.uk/rds/index.html

where many of our publications are available to be read on screen or downloaded for printing.